The Blue Wave
Starts with Me

A Volunteer's Guide to
Getting Out the Vote for Democrats

Ron Boyer

To a community organizer who gave us hope and to the millions of volunteers who made him president.

CONTENTS

No matter how hard the loss, defeat might serve as well as victory to shake the soul and let the glory out.

Al Gore

INTRODUCTION

Up until the election in 2000, electoral politics was a spectator sport for me. I loved to read about politics. I loved to watch. I voted.

And then Al Gore lost by a few dozen votes. Since then I have lived with the belief that if there had been one more volunteer in the State of Florida in 2000, we would not have gone to war in Iraq, we would not have crashed the economy, and we would have made a whole lot more progress in addressing global warming. So I have tried to arrange my life to be able, from time to time, to volunteer to get out the vote for Democrats.

And I have no regrets. It has been such a pleasure to meet Democratic voters and people who are motivated to give a little of their time to help get out the vote. And it has been so satisfying to be part of these campaigns, each of which has been so important. It is, of course, more satisfying to be part of a winning effort. But we won't win every election. And if we are going to lose, it is much better to feel that one was part of the effort to try to win than to have been on the sidelines.

After the election in 2016, there are more than a few people feeling the way that I did in 2000. People who have never volunteered with a campaign before are saying to themselves that they are not going to sit out 2018 and they are not going to sit out 2020. This book is for them.

The purpose of this book is to make it easier for people like that to get involved.

I have good news: you can make a difference. Volunteers have a critical role to play in increasing voter turnout. The research shows that volunteers, with just a little training, can be especially good at it, better than people who are paid to do it.

You do not need to be an expert. It is enough if you are sincere and kind and motivated. There is a place for you whether you have a little time to give or a lot. Campaigns are grateful for people who can put in a lot of time. But movements are built with the efforts of lots and lots of people who can put in a little time.

If you have a little time to give and you are motivated to help get Democratic voters to the polls, especially if you have never done anything like this before, this book is for you.

Now let me be the first to thank you. It is people like you who give me hope. Together we can do this.

It is common sense to take a method and try it. If it fails, admit it frankly and try another. But above all, try something.

Franklin D. Roosevelt

1 MONEYBALL

You might have seen the movie *Moneyball* or read the book by the same name. You might know the story.

For over a hundred years baseball had been played by rules of thumb. Old guys knew from experience the right way to play the game and they passed it on to new players. And old, experienced guys were charged with watching younger players as they played and determining who was worthy of a chance at playing professionally.

Then in the 1990's some people started to run statistics to determine which of the choices a team might make, in the drafting of players or in the playing of the game, actually lead to winning more baseball games. And some of those rules of thumb turned out to be wrong.

But because there were plenty of people managing baseball teams who believed in those rules of thumb, this created an opportunity for someone who was willing to make decisions based on the statistics, even when it was in the face of howls of protest from more experienced hands.

Billy Bean, the general manager of the Oakland Athletics, was able to assemble and manage a team that for a period of about seven years in the early 2000's won more regular season games than any team other than the New York Yankees and they trailed the Yankees over that time period by only a handful of games. Moreover, the Oakland Athletics did this with one of the smallest budgets in baseball while the New York Yankees had the largest.

The same sort of thing is true in political campaigns. For over a hundred years campaigns had been run by rules of thumb. Old, experienced guys would come in and say, "We have done this before. We know what to do. We'll put together a campaign for you, the whole package."

And then in the 1990's a couple of professors at Yale started gathering statistics on what was actually effective at getting voters to the polls. And some of those rules of thumb turned out to be wrong.

What they learned was that, of the things that a campaign can control, the single most effective thing at increasing a voter's probability of going to the polls is a face-to-face conversation with a volunteer. The second most effective thing is a phone call with a volunteer. And everything else is dramatically less effective.

They learned that a campaign can pour money into television, into radio ads, into robo calls, into mailers, into emails, into billboards, into yard signs—even into paying people to make calls and knock on doors—and none of it has anything like the effect of a real, human conversation between a voter and someone who is not being paid to have that conversation, who is doing it out of love and commitment.

You will notice something about this. Because it is based on volunteers, it is something that money can't buy. It requires money. You need money to maintain databases, to open field offices, to buy supplies. But by definition, you can't buy a volunteer. If a campaign does not have a lot of people who believe in the campaign and believe in the candidate, this is not a tool that is available at any price.

We should be clear about the limitations of this. We are talking about the effect of things that a campaign can do. There are things that the campaign cannot control. We cannot control the state of the economy or the time in history. We cannot control the opposition. But of the things that a campaign can control, nothing is more effective at increasing our chances of victory than what you as a volunteer can provide. Second to the candidate, no one is more valuable to a campaign than someone like you who cares enough to give some of their time.

I first saw this used by MoveOn in the congressional races of 2006. With the advent of widespread internet access and cell phone plans with unlimited national calling, volunteers everywhere in the country were engaged in getting out the vote in key congressional races anywhere in the country. Barack Obama's campaign fully embraced it in 2008. In 2008, more than two million people volunteered with the Obama campaign. It is no accident that a community organizer became president.

Now the research has marched on since the 1990's, though not as much as you might think. Partly the ability to do research is limited by the fact that there are only so many elections. Including 2006, there have been six congressional elections since 2006. There have been three presidential elections since that time. And there have been additional state and local elections. This is not like baseball where in the major leagues each team plays 162 games a year. The number of times that we get to run these experiments is much more limited.

So I have to throw in the caveat. It is impossible for everything we do to be based on data. Some of what we do has to be based on experience and judgment and instinct.

Where there is research, we use it. Where there is no research, we do our best. And, fortunately, people in the Democratic Party and their allies have gotten quite good at this.

What you are getting in this book is the lessons of the research mingled with my own experience. (If you want to know more of who I am, take a peek at the biographical note at the back of the book.) By the time you get to a campaign, there may be new and better research. There may be people organizing who have more experience and different insights. I believe that what you get in this book is nonetheless a pretty representative look at what we are going to be asking of you as a volunteer. It is your introduction. It is the beginning, not the end.

The bottom line is that while we have learned a few things from the research since 2006 and 2008 and 2012 and 2016, this basic fact remains true: volunteers who will knock on doors and make phone calls can make a difference of about three to five percent in voter turnout. And while that may not seem like a lot, it is enough to win a lot of elections that would otherwise be lost.

And it all starts with people with no more knowledge or experience than you. It starts with people who care and who can give a little of their time. It starts with me. It starts with you.

Our greatest strength comes not from what we possess, but from what we believe; not from what we have, but from who we are.

Michael Dukakis

2 PEOPLE LIKE TO BE ASKED

While the research and the data that show the power of these techniques is new, there is nothing new about canvassing and phone banking. The basic premise is that we are going to go out and ask people for their vote.

Remember Tip O'Neill? For those who are young enough not to know who Tip O'Neill was, he represented a Massachusetts district in the House of Representatives from 1963 to 1987 and was Speaker of the House from 1977 to 1987. And if you are old enough to remember Tip O'Neill, you might just remember this story.

In his first campaign for public office, in 1934, Tip O'Neill was a senior at Boston College running for a seat on the Cambridge City Counsel. On the last day of the campaign he ran into Elizabeth O'Brien, his neighbor from across the street who had also been a teacher of his in high school.

She said, "Tom, I'm going to vote for you tomorrow even though you didn't ask me."

"But Mrs. O'Brien," he said, "I shovel your sidewalk in winter, I mow your grass in summer, and I take out your trash twice a week, I didn't think I had to ask for your vote."

She said, "Tom, let me tell you something. People like to be asked."

Change will not come if we wait for some other person or some other time. We are the ones we've been waiting for. We are the change that we seek.

Barack Obama

3 WHO CAN VOLUNTEER?

Of course the answer to that is anyone can volunteer. But it needs a little emphasis. So forgive me if I repeat myself just a little.

Not everyone has a lot of time to give. Mostly, we have jobs. We have children to care for. We have elderly parents to care for. We do other volunteer work and have people who depend on us. We have real lives. We have commitments.

Without a doubt campaigns appreciate the efforts of people who can give a lot of time. But campaigns can only achieve the scale to make a real difference through the efforts of lots and lots of people who can give only a little time.

If you can volunteer only on the weekend before Election Day, you can still make a big difference. If you can make plans to take a day off work on Election Day and volunteer that day, too, so much the better.

If you can give four hours on a weekend once a month, you are the kind of person that is the backbone of the campaign. It is by having lots and lots of people like you that our campaign becomes a movement.

This is the ground game. It is three yards and a cloud of dust. Each of us volunteering can increase voter turnout out by only a tiny bit. But when we each do the little bit that we can do, we can make a big difference.

One volunteer giving four hours of time does not seem like much. But a hundred volunteers each giving four hours of time is four hundred hours. It is hard for a campaign to get four hundred hours of work in some way other than all those volunteers who can just give four hours. In a national presidential campaign there may be more than a million volunteers. Then we are taking about four million hours. You can get a lot done in four million hours.

*Young people have so much more power than they
tend to think to be able to affect politics. And if people
will organize and get involved and go out and knock
on doors and hand out leaflets and make a change,
then they can determine the future.*

John Kerry

4 THE STRUCTURE OF A CAMPAIGN, BACKWARDS

Who ya gonna call?

On Election Day, or during early voting, we are calling voters and knocking on the doors of voters and asking them to get to the polls. Classic get out the vote. Call it "GOTV" and sound like an old pro at this.

Who do we want to contact? We want to contact supporters who are occasional voters.

How you vote is secret. Whether you vote is public record. From these public records the campaigns can assemble a database that identifies in which of the preceding elections a voter has cast a ballot. We can tell

11

who votes in every election. We can tell who votes only in presidential elections. We can tell who almost never votes.

We don't put our efforts into reaching the people who always vote. Nor are we trying to talk to the people who never vote. We want to talk to the people who vote some of the time because a little nudge from us is more likely to get them to the polls. We try to talk to the people where our little nudges are most likely to make a difference.

And, of course, we try to be reaching supporters. The people who we want to get to the polls are the people who are likely to vote for our candidate.

So what are we doing before election day?

Before voting begins we are out there knocking on doors and making calls. What are we doing?

Identifying our supporters.

Job one prior to GOTV is trying to identify our supporters. Every time we talk to a person on the phone or at their front door we make a record of how likely we think they are to vote for our candidate. These records will help us more accurately identify who we want to get to the polls.

Hey, I got another wrong number!

Another priority prior to getting out the vote is cleaning up our lists. People move. Their phone numbers change. There are always lots of wrong numbers. That's just the nature of modern life. But every time you reach a wrong number or a number that has been disconnected you are helping the campaign by getting that number off the list. Every time in advance of Election Day that you reach a wrong number or a number that has been disconnected, that means that we will not waste time calling that number on Election Day. Every time you reach a wrong number in advance of Election Day, that means that we will be able to reach one more live voter on Election Day.

Registering voters.

Even earlier in the campaign cycle we are registering new voters. If you have time to give to a campaign well in advance of Election Day, it may be too soon to know who our supporters will be and it may be too soon to have the conversations that increase their chances of getting voters to the polls, but it can be extremely valuable to Democratic campaigns to increase voter registration.

Persuasion calls? Not so much.

It may seem odd, but one of the things that we do not use volunteers for is changing people's minds. Up through the 2012 campaign we would make calls that were intended to persuade undecided voters. What we learned is that volunteers making phone calls was not an effective way to do this. We were as likely to push people the other way as pull them our way.

Persuading people how to vote is a job for the candidate. Undecided voters might be influenced by the news or by talking to their friends. And you might be effective at changing the minds of the people who know you well and respect you. But, for the most part, an undecided voter is not going to make up their mind based on getting a phone call from someone they have never met.

As volunteers, we can be very effective at getting people to vote. We can be very effective at registering new voters. We are not so effective at influencing how people will vote.

A virtuous pyramid scheme.

Throughout the arc of the campaign we are recruiting volunteers. Say one day you make a bunch of calls and recruit three volunteers. And the following week, those three volunteers come in and the four of you make calls and each recruit three more volunteers. And the following week the 16 of you come in and make a bunch of calls and each recruit three more volunteers.

You can see where this is heading. We are continuously building our campaign.

Come Election Day, across the nation, there may be a couple of million people volunteering to get out the vote. It all starts with a few phone calls.

If you are lucky enough to get involved at the beginning of a campaign, you will get to see this. Sometimes the first phone bank will have just one person making calls. I have done that. The first meeting might be five people. It might be two. If those two people are sincere and kind and motivated, they will soon be joined by more people like that.

The other thing about this that you should know is that volunteers are like voters in this: they like to be asked. Some people are just waiting for that call from someone asking them to help and when they get it they will jump in with both feet. So I am asking you right now, can you help us?

You can do what you have to do, and sometimes you can do it even better than you think you can.

Jimmy Carter

5 WHAT DO YOU SAY?

Follow the script. Don't follow the script.

Almost always when you canvass or when you phone bank the campaign will give you a script as to what they want you to say. And the people who organize our campaigns have good reasons for wanting you to follow the script. The research shows that when we say certain kinds of things they are more effective at increasing voter turnout than when we say other kinds of things.

At the same time, we want you to have a real human conversation. The fact that you are a person who cares enough to give your time and that you are having a back-and-forth conversation with a voter is a big part of what makes you effective at increasing voter turnout. If you are reading a script, you are robbing yourself of some of the authenticity of your personal presence.

What to do?

I believe that in any real conversation, even if you wanted to follow the script, you would rarely get to. Some conversations are shorter. Some conversations are longer. Having a real conversation means responding to the person you are talking to.

When I train volunteers, I train them in the kinds of things that are in the scripts, and then I encourage them to have a real conversation. The idea is to put as many of these things into your conversation as you can fit in naturally without forcing it.

"I am a volunteer."

You will want to identify yourself as a volunteer at the outset. "Hi, I am Ron Boyer, I am a volunteer for Kamala Harris." Why this?

The research shows that volunteers are much more effective at increasing voter turnout than paid canvassers. When you identify yourself as a volunteer you get the benefit of that. You let the voter know that you are not there just because you are paid to be there; you are there because you care enough to give your time.

By identifying yourself as a volunteer you increase the chance that your conversation will result in that voter going to the polls.

"We are calling voters like you."

When we identify the person we are talking to as a voter, we encourage them to identify themselves as a voter and, the research shows, this increases the probability that they will vote. So the scripts that you get will often, in one way or another, use the word "voter" to refer to the person you are talking to. And if you use the word "voter," in one way or another, to refer to that person, you increase the probability that the person you are talking to will go to the polls and be a voter.

"Can we count on you going to the polls and voting on Election Day?"

If a voter will make to you a promise to vote, the research shows that doubles the impact of your conversation. If with one kind of wording or another you can get the voter to promise to vote, you have doubled the chance that they will actually go to the polls and vote. That is why you will see that kind of language in your scripts. That is why, if you can and it comes naturally, you want to put that kind of language into your conversation.

"Can we count on you to vote this year no matter what?"

"Can we count on you to return your mail ballot this week?"

"Will you make a pledge to vote on November 8th?"

"Can we count on you to be one of the first in line to vote this Tuesday?"

"It looks as though turnout is going to be high."

When it is true, we want to tell voters that the turnout is going to be high. Research shows that people are more likely to vote if they believe that turnout is going to be high than if they believe that turnout is going to be low.

When it is true, I will say, "We are expecting a big turnout. There might be lines. You might want to get there early."

"It looks as though this race is going to be close. Your vote is going to make a difference."

Again, when it is true, we want to tell voters that the race is going to be close. Research shows that when people believe the race is close they are more likely to vote than if they believe that the race is not close.

For your own sake, and for theirs, remember that all polls come with a margin of error. Anyone who lived through 2016 will never forget that races that seem like a sure thing can turn out not to be. Even when the polls show that we are ahead, it does not mean a thing unless people actually take the trouble to show up and vote.

Sometimes I will say, "We are pretty sure that the support is there. If everyone who supports us actually shows up and votes then we are going to win."

Or you might say, if it is true, "This race is within the margin of error. It is as a close to a dead heat as it can be. Your vote could be the difference this time."

Walk them through a plan to vote.

"Will you vote early, vote by mail, or vote on Election Day?"

"Do you know where your polling place is?"

"Do you know how you are going to get there? Do you need a ride?"

"Will you vote in the morning or in the evening?"

"Are there other people in your household who will vote at the same time?"

The research shows that it doubles the impact of your conversation if you can walk the voter through a concrete vision of what is entailed in voting. You do this by asking questions and getting them to formulate a plan to vote.

Again, if you can naturally work this into your conversation, that voter is twice as likely to get to the polls.

Would it be alright to call you back after Election Day?

Sometimes campaigns will put some volunteer effort into making follow-up calls after Election Day. I would like to see a few more phone banks scheduled *after* Election Day. Asking about this in advance can increase voter turnout.

So when this is true you can say something like:

"Our campaign is interested in the experiences that voters have at the polls. Would it be alright for someone to call you back after Election Day to ask you how it went? Is this the best number to reach you at?"

Something we don't say.

Oddly the research says that it is counterproductive to give a reason for voting. If we say something like, "It's important to vote because of the environment," or "It's important to vote because of the economy," or "It's important to vote because of the Supreme Court," or any other specific policy reason, that actually decreases voter turnout.

Treat people kindly.

Respect, love and kindness are at the core of what it means to be a Democrat. You are the personal manifestation of that.

So be considerate. If people don't have time, they are in a hurry, the baby is crying, the dinner's on the stove, don't impose. Or maybe they are watching the football game on TV, same thing. In such circumstances, your interaction may be exceedingly brief. That you are kind and considerate may be the core of your message.

"Hi, I'm just a volunteer with Elizabeth Warren's campaign. I just came by to ask for your vote. We can come back another time."

"We're just out reminding people that Election Day is Tuesday. Don't forget to vote. Now get back to the game, but first tell me the score."

Being kind and considerate and keeping it short is probably what is going to help the campaign the most under those circumstances.

People who are against us? Treat them kindly, too.

Not everyone supports our candidate. I know that comes as a shock. Almost all of the people who you talk to will be supporters because the basic premise of our lists is that we are trying to get our supporters to the polls. But you will on occasion knock on the door of or ring the phone of someone who is against us.

Do not argue with people. It saps your spirit, it takes your time, and it does not help the campaign.

When you meet someone who is against us, listen respectfully, disengage kindly, move on with the task at hand. Your task is to go find the next supporter and ask them to get out and vote.

What about undecided voters?

As a general proposition, canvassers and phone bankers

are not the ones who are going to change the minds of voters about who to vote for. People like to make up their own minds and it is rarely an unknown person at the door or on the phone that is going to be the difference in that.

So if someone is undecided, be empathetic, be respectful, don't push.

I say that if a voter is truly undecided (as opposed to someone who just does not want to tell you how they are going to vote), go ahead and encourage them to vote and don't worry how they are going to vote. They have been demographically targeted as being a likely voter for your candidate. You can say something like, "We would like to get your vote on election day, but whether you vote for our candidate or not, I still want to encourage you to get the polls and be a part of the process."

Why should I vote for [insert your candidate's name here]?

Sometime people will ask for a reason. This is your chance to tell your story.

A standard practice in the Obama campaign was to have volunteers meet in a circle and go around and introduce themselves by telling their own story. What brings you here? What in your life motivated you to come out and give your time to this candidate? Sometimes it is a personal story about health care or about opportunity or about your grandchildren or your grandmother or some policy that you think and care about or something that the candidate said or did. Sometimes it is something else entirely. There is something that motivates you personally.

Sometimes we would like to think that we should be experts on all kinds of policy. We should know the candidate's position on every last issue. We should know what we think, ourselves, about every last issue. I think hardly anyone does. Most of us have jobs and family and commitments that mean that we cannot spend enough time thinking about public policy to be experts. At the same time there are things in our lives and in the news that we do think about and care about. And those things motivate us to act. They motivate us to get out and do something and make a difference. Take a moment to pause and think about those things are in your life. And think about how, in a minute or so, you can tell your story. Why are you here? Why do you care about this election?

Barack Obama is not on the ballot, so imagine you are helping get out the vote for Congressman Conor Lamb in Western Pennsylvania. When you are at the front door or on the phone you are ready for this question. When they ask you, "Why should I vote for Conor Lamb," the answer is, "I can't tell you why you should vote for Conor Lamb, but here is why I am voting for Conor Lamb."

And when you tell that story, implicit in that is the message of "and here is why I am giving up my free time on a Saturday to make phone calls and knock doors for Conor Lamb." In the end, your actions speak louder than your words.

As we express our gratitude, we must never forget that the highest appreciation is not to utter words, but to live by them.

John F. Kennedy

6 WHAT DO I SAY?

The last chapter was based on research. This chapter is my totally-personal approach.

When I was going door to door in New Mexico in 2008, my dialogue went like this:

"Hi, I'm Ron Boyer, a volunteer with the Obama campaign. How are you today?"

We might engage in just a little pleasantry and then I would say, "I'm here to ask for your vote for Barack Obama."

Why this?

First of all, I should say that campaigns often want you to ask in one way or another how people are going to vote. That is important because it is are supporters who we want to get to the polls.

At the same time many people, I believe especially in battleground states, take the secret ballot seriously. If you are asking them *how* they are going to vote, you are invading their privacy. It can seem a little rude to walk up to a stranger and ask them how they are going to vote.

But if you ask *for* their vote, you are treating them with respect. They have the power to do something important. We want them to do it. It is polite to ask.

Secondly, you get the same information. The campaign is trying to identify supporters. When I say, "I'm here to ask for your vote for Kirsten Gillibrand," or "I'm here to ask for your vote for Cory Booker," the answer is going to be "You got it," or "No way," or something else. Almost always they are going to tell you how they are going to vote. If not, if they do not give an answer when you ask them for their vote, then I am pretty sure they were not going to tell you if you asked them directly. Sometimes, when I have a friendly response, but they don't quite answer, I follow up with "What are the chances?"

If they are a supporter, and if I get the chance, I will move into the kind of things that I discussed in the last chapter. I will get a promise to vote. I will walk them through a plan to vote. If we expect the turnout to be high or the race to be close, I will talk about that.

At the outset, however, I believe that the most persuasive thing you can do is to be a kind person who shows their commitment by volunteering for the campaign and who politely asks for their vote. The research shows that nothing is more effective in terms of increasing voter turnout than a face-to-face conversation with a volunteer. Close behind is a phone call from a volunteer. What is it that makes the difference? I don't believe it is arguments or policies or data nearly so much as it is just the presence of a reasonable, respectful human being who isn't being paid to talk to them but is doing it out of their own commitment. Once you have introduced yourself and said that line, "I'm here to ask for your vote for Eric Holder," you have done all that in a nutshell. While your conversation may go on or it may not, your basic task is complete.

For me, this basic conversation is also kind of a joke and I try to let it show in the tone of my voice that it is kind of a joke. I just told them I am from the Obama Campaign. So what could I possibly be calling about? "I'm here to ask for your vote for Barack Obama" is a way of just stating the obvious. ["Well Duh!"] So state it with the positive tone that you would put on a punch line: cheerfulness mingled with a little pride and the little bit of intimacy that comes from expecting them to get the joke. It's your one-liner.

Finally, it is a way of cutting to the chase that lets people know that you are not wasting their time and you are not here to lecture them or to argue with them. People in battleground states get polled and pestered a lot. You are just here to ask. You are going to ask right up front. And then, unless they really want to talk, you are going to go away again. I think that if you say, "I'm here to ask for your vote for Joe Biden," right up front after you introduce yourself, you communicate all that, too. You have put them at the ease of knowing that if they politely want to end the conversation and go on with their day, that's no problem; you aren't going to pressure them to talk or to listen longer.

That is the gist of what we are about here. As a volunteer, your job is just to go out and knock on doors, or call on the phone, and politely ask people for their vote.

RON BOYER

*Patriotism is not short, frenzied outbursts of emotion,
but the tranquil and steady dedication of a lifetime.*

Adlai Stevenson

7 NOBODY IS HOME

Mostly people are not home.

Whenever we call, there are going to be a lot of people not home. Typical is 85 percent not home.

That means that there is a premium on dialing through the numbers to reach the people who are home. It is good to set yourself up in a way where you can dial the phone efficiently. I like to use a headset on my cell phone because then the phone is always in front of me. A lot of what you are going to be doing is dialing and dialing again. So put a little thought into making this easy for yourself.

Four rings and move on.

I have not seen research on this, but I am going to give you a rule of thumb. I learned it from an old union activist who was probably making GOTV calls before I was born. Let it ring four times and if no one answers hang up and move on to the next number. Sometimes your call list will show the age of the voter and if you are calling someone who is elderly enough that they might have mobility problems you might let it ring a couple of more times. But otherwise, that old union guy and I think that the number of people who will answer after four rings is small enough that you will reach more people, total, if you hang up after four rings and move on.

We don't leave messages.

You might think that if we have made all the effort to call someone, we should leave a message on their voice mail or answering machine. Surely that is a positive thing. What could be the harm? There are two reasons we don't leave messages.

The first one is that the research shows that messages don't increase voter turnout. That means that if you are leaving messages you are putting a lot of time into doing something that is not actually helping the campaign. You will dial a lot more numbers if you don't leave messages. And if you dial a lot more numbers you will have a lot more of the conversations that the research shows will actually increase voter turnout.

The second reason we do not leave messages is that if no one answers the phone you are going to code that call as "not home." That means that someone else will be calling back that number soon. And that means that if we leave messages when people are not home we are going to leave lots of messages. Instead of leaving one message on an answering machine we could very quickly leave a dozen messages on the answering machine. And that would not be a good thing.

There are rare occasions and special circumstances when campaigns will ask phone bankers to leave messages. One example is when there is a local event where the candidate is coming to town. So if the campaign specifically asks you to leave messages on voice mail and answering machines, then by all means do so.

Otherwise, whenever you hear the voice mail or answering machine pick up, hang up and move on to the next call. You will be doing more to help the campaign.

RON BOYER

If you are sure you understand everything that is going on, you are hopelessly confused.

Walter Mondale

8 CODING IS IMPORTANT

Coding is important.

All the calls we make, in addition to giving nudges that get voters to the polls, give the campaign information that helps us do a better job of getting out the vote ... but only if we record that information accurately.

When we make calls or knock on doors we will have a place to enter the results of each attempt, either on a paper sheet or on a smart phone or on a computer. One way or another there will be boxes to check or numbers to circle to show the results of your work.

That being so, it is important to know how each of the possible responses are defined. In different campaigns and at different times the possible answers are set up differently. So this is one area where you are just going to have to get the details in an orientation with whatever campaign you volunteer with. Some codes, like "not home," will be completely obvious. Others will be not so obvious. When they tell you how to code your results, pay attention.

There are, however, a couple of other things that I can say about coding.

Write clearly

I say this as someone with terrible handwriting. I do my best, but please do better than me. Write so people can read what you wrote. Mark the boxes with large, clear marks. Circle them if that makes it clearer.

Also, if possible, use a pen with ink that is blue or some color other than black so that it is easy to see on the black-and-white call sheets or canvass sheets.

Finally, it is a good idea to put your name and cell phone number at the top of each page that you do. This makes it easy for someone who is entering data to call you up and ask if there is any doubt.

When in doubt, make a note.

If you are at all unsure about how to code something, make a note explaining what the situation is. This will allow campaign organizers or data people to make a decision as to how best to code the information or follow up.

You can also write a note whenever a voter tells you something that you think the campaign would want to know that does not fit cleanly into your coding options.

Notes are good.

Don't code second hand results.

Sometimes at the door or on the phone you will reach someone who is not the voter on your list, but who will tell you with confidence what that voter is going to do. Almost all the time you should code that as "not home."

So when you are making calls for Deval Patrick and you call a voter named "Mary," if a man answers and says, "Mary's not here, but don't worry, she will be voting for Deval Patrick," you code that as "not home." The reason for this is that we want another volunteer to try again on another day so that we might actually have the conversation that is going to increase the chances of getting that voter to the polls.

Conversely if a man answers and says, "Mary's not here, but don't waste your time, we are all voting for the other guy," you have to code that as "not home." Why? People who are supporters are sometimes living with or married to people who are not supporters. In particular, there is often a big gender gap. With respect to Obama, with respect to Hillary, with respect to a lot of Democratic candidates, we have had substantially more support among women than among men. And that means that often women who support us are married to or in relationships with men who do not support us. It is less common, but it can go the other way, too. Moreover, often enough in couples like this, they do not talk about the difference for the sake of the relationship. When they are telling you something like, "Don't waste your time," there is nothing to be gained by being confrontational about it. Just say, "thank you" and code "not home."

A pessimist is one who makes difficulties of his opportunities and an optimist is one who makes opportunities of his difficulties.

Harry Truman

9 BUT I DON'T WANT TO MAKE PHONE CALLS OR KNOCK ON DOORS.

Maybe you hate to make phone calls. Maybe you cannot imagine yourself walking up to a stranger's door and knocking. And yet you want to help. What are you going to do?

The good news is that there are lots of ways to help.

Registering voters

As a general proposition, the more people who vote, the better the results for Democrats. A key goal for the Democratic party, then, is increasing the electorate. That means registering voters. Some people find the conversations to be had in registering voters are easier for them than the conversations that go with GOTV.

Volunteers are organized to set up tables or carry clip boards in public places such as in front of supermarkets, at fairs or at farmer's markets. Sometimes volunteers will go to the swearing-in ceremonies for new citizens and register voters there.

You will want to be sure to be well trained so that you are complying with the law of your state. But whether you also get involved in GOTV or not, consider volunteering time to register voters.

Texting and writing post cards

There has been research that shows that there are certain age groups that respond well to reminders to vote that come by text message. That means that some campaigns will organize volunteers to send text messages to voters in those age groups.

Also, although I have not seen research regarding how effective it is, there are groups who organize volunteers to write personalized post cards to voters. Some of these are quite artistic. Certainly hand written post cards must stand out and be more memorable than typical campaign mail.

These are each less personal than a face-to-face conversation or a phone call, but they are more personal than other forms of campaign contact. If this appeals to you, it is definitely worth doing.

Support for other volunteers.

It is still the case that what is going to make the most difference to the campaign is maximizing the number of person-to-person contacts between volunteers and potential voters. If you are not going to be one of the volunteers, you can still be doing things that will maximize those contacts.

A comfortable place to be.

One key need is a place to hold phone banks. Phone banks do not need to be large in order to be effective. Your home does not need to be large in order to host a phone bank.

It takes some time and work to clean up your house and make it ready to host callers. It takes some time and work to clean up again after they leave. People who are ready to make calls may not have the time and energy to host a phone bank in their home. Or maybe their families feel that they are giving enough to the campaign and they do not want the additional disturbance of having other callers come around. My children as teenagers felt that way. So if we can hold the phone bank at your house, it makes a big difference and makes it a lot easier for everyone.

Another aspect of this is that the more different homes we can hold phone banks in, the more people will come to our phone banks. Some people will go anywhere. But not everyone is comfortable everywhere. Some people are not comfortable going to a neighborhood where people are much richer than they are. Some people are not comfortable going to a neighborhood where people are much poorer than they are. Some people will go to a phone bank in their own neighborhood but are less likely to go to a phone bank that is five miles away. Some people would rather go to a campaign office of some kind. Other people are more likely to show up at an event in a private home or a local cafe. These people all might happily work together, but some of them are comfortable in one space and some in another. So the more different kinds of spaces we can make available to people, the more people will get involved.

Maybe you have access to a space other than your home at which you can host a phone bank. Maybe you have a cafe or an office. Maybe you are a member of a club or a union or a school or some other organization that has a space that you can use. Maybe you live in an apartment building or a condo that has a community space that you can use. If you can make the arrangements to use that space, to set up before and clean up after, again that is a big help to the campaign. And that will mean that more volunteers will have more of those conversations that we know are going to increase voter turnout.

Being the host of a venue like this does not mean that you need to run the phone bank. There are other volunteers in the campaign, or paid staff, who can organize the call lists and train the volunteers and all of that sort of thing. But if you can provide a space, you are making their job much easier.

If volunteers have a place where they feel comfortable and welcome, then they are more likely to show up and they are more likely to come back. And if volunteers have a place where they feel comfortable and welcome, then they are going to have a better attitude on the phone and have better conversations that are more effective at getting voters to the polls. So if you can provide a space for phone banks, you can make an important contribution to the campaign.

Something to eat.

It makes a big difference to a campaign to have good food to feed volunteers. They might be going out to canvass. They might be phone banking. They might be working in one way or another in a campaign office or staging location.

Often there is neither a lot of time or money to put into feeding people. I see a lot of pizza. I see a lot of coffee. If people show up with homemade food, that is a huge plus.

We do not want our volunteers to be low blood sugar. We don't want them walking around hungry. Campaigns can be very stressful. Good, healthy food can help to keep everyone healthy through the stress.

So if you can bring in some good, healthy food for people to eat, you can raise morale. You can make those volunteers more chipper. You can make them smarter and more resilient. You can make them better volunteers. The conversations that they have with voters will be better conversations and more effective at increasing voter turnout.

So if you are not one who is ready to talk to voters, but you can cook, there is an important role for you.

Data entry.

When canvassers go out knocking on doors, they usually take paper sheets upon which they record the results of their efforts. Coding. Who was home? Who has moved? Who is a supporter? Who has made a commitment to get to the polls? Who wants to volunteer?

All of this information has to get back into the database so that it can be used in the next round of contacts.

Some people who are not ready to knock on doors or make phone calls are people who are comfortable with their computers and comfortable entering data into a database. If you are one of those people, then that is an important way that you can help.

It is true that there are some apps for smart phones that allow canvassers to put the data straight into the database rather than onto a paper sheet on a clip board. But not everyone who is ready to knock on doors is comfortable using that kind of technology. So if we have people who will do the data entry, we make it easier for more people to canvass.

It is also true that there are computer applications that allow phone bankers to enter the results from their calls directly into the database. But again, not everyone who is comfortable make calls is necessarily comfortable and adept at using a computer. So again, if we have people entering data for these people, we make it possible for more volunteers to make more calls.

There is another factor with respect to phone banking. Whether or not you are adept at using your computer, it is generally quicker to record the results of a phone call on a paper sheet than it is to enter it into the computer. That means that when callers use paper sheets they make more phone calls and they have more of the conversations that will increase voter turnout. And the only way that those volunteers can do that is if there is someone else, someone who would not otherwise be making calls, taking the paper sheets and entering the data into the system.

So, if you can volunteer by entering data, even if you are not someone who will make phone calls, you can be helping the campaign have more of the conversations that we know will increase voter turnout.

Driving canvassers.

When we think about getting out the vote, we often think of driving voters to the polls. While there are voters who appreciate a ride to the polls, in my experience there is less need for this than you might think. But there is another role for drivers.

When we are knocking on doors we are not knocking on every door. Our lists are targeted for people who are likely to be supporters but whom public records show to be occasional voters. Especially in suburban or rural areas, there may be a significant distance between houses. That means that it is often not efficient to just walk from one house to the next.

If a canvasser is out on their own, then they may find themselves getting in and out of the car as they drive from one targeted door or cluster of doors to another. A person who is not ready to have those conversations at the door might have a car and be ready to drive.

With a separate driver, the person who is canvassing can be much more efficient. They can just hop out and go to the door while the driver stays behind the wheel. There is less time lost parking. There is less time lost setting aside your clip board and starting up the car.

So if you have a car and are comfortable driving, you can help increase the number of personal contacts that research shows will increase voter turnout by driving canvassers as they make their rounds.

Personal notes.

This is a nice touch that I first saw in Western Pennsylvania when I was getting out the vote for Conor Lamb's campaign for Congress in March of 2018.

For a substantial percentage of the doors that we knock on, no one is home. Much of the time the campaign will have a door hanger or some other kind of literature that we leave who were not home when we came by.

This literature is glossy and can be effective. But it can be much more effective with a personal, handwritten note. Here is a note that is representative of the notes written for Conor Lamb's campaign.

> Hello,
> Sorry I missed you.
> I hope you will vote in the <u>Special Election</u> on <u>Tuesday, March 13th.</u>

The polls open at 7:00 A.M. & close at 8:00 P.M. Thank you.

Personally, I have terrible handwriting. But if you have legible handwriting, you can help the campaign to increase voter turnout by writing notes like this and sticking them on the literature that is going to be left by canvassers.

Other kinds of calls.

The lists of people who we call to recruit volunteers are a little different from the lists of people who we call to get out the vote. They are more likely to be supporters and pretty enthusiastic supporters at that. So some people who are not ready to call voters find it easy to make volunteer-recruitment calls.

And then there are reminder calls. For any event that we hold, any canvass, any phone bank, any other event, there is a certain percentage of people who will sign up but then not show up. This is referred to charmingly as the "flake rate."

If we call people who have signed up and give them a little reminder in advance of the event—"I see you are signed up for the phone bank tomorrow at 1:00, thank you so much!"—we increase the number of people who actually show up. And some people who are not ready to call voters find it easy to make this kind of reminder call.

The Gandhi

Gandhi famously took upon himself one of the least honored chores and turned it into one of the most honorable: he cleaned the latrines.

In 2012, in Berkeley, California, we were holding phone

banks with dozens of volunteers in a building that had been an auto repair garage. It had one small bathroom.

The experience of these volunteers was vastly improved by the fact that there were a couple of volunteers who took on the task of making sure that bathroom stayed clean.

And because those volunteers took on that role, we can be sure that many more people showed up and stayed and were of much better cheer than if no one had taken on that role.

We treated those volunteers with the highest level of respect that we could bestow.

A place for travelers.

Some volunteers will travel a long distance to volunteer. If you live in a battleground state during a presidential election, or in a congressional district with a key congressional race, there are likely to be people from other states and districts who want to come knock on doors and help get out the vote. If you can make a spare bedroom available to a volunteer like that, you can make it much easier for volunteers to come in and do that.

The bottom line.

The research shows that one of the most effective things that a campaign can do to increase voter turnout is a one-to-one conversation with a volunteer. If you are someone who can have those conversations, then that is what you should do. Knock on doors. Make calls.

If that is not you, then think about what you can do to support the people who are having those conversations. Give them a space. Feed them. Make their task easier in any way that you can.

And one other thing: thank them. Every volunteer that you meet, show your appreciation. Thank them for being there. And thank you for being there. Thank you for everything that you do to help turn out the vote for Democrats. Together we can do what we can't do alone.

The highest patriotism is not a blind acceptance of official policy, but a love of one's country deep enough to call her to a higher plain.

George McGovern

10 I'M FIRED UP! WHERE DO I GO?

With whom should I volunteer?

There is a broad and happy diversity of Democratic Party organizations and allies of the Democratic Party that are doing this work. You have many choices. You do not have to stick to one organization.

Any particular contact information I might put here may quickly go out of date. Still, it should not be too hard to find a way to volunteer, either locally or on line. For any candidate or organization that you might volunteer for, you can almost certainly find them with an Internet search on the name of the candidate or organization, perhaps with the additional word "volunteer."

Volunteer with a candidate's campaign.

The biggest operations of this kind are the presidential campaigns. It is very exciting and important to be part of a presidential campaign. I definitely recommend that.

But you should not wait for a presidential campaign to get involved. You can volunteer with a campaign for any candidate who you believe in, whether they are running for the United States Senate or Congress, for governor or the state legislature, for county commissioner or city council. All campaigns will have a get out the vote element and you can be part of it.

Volunteer with the Democratic Party.

There are other national Democratic Party organizations that may be involved in organizing GOTV. Your state Democratic Party may organize a coordinated campaign to get out the vote for candidates up and down the ballot. You might also try getting in touch with the Democratic Party organization for your county. Some counties are more active and organized than others. Who is actually doing this at any time may vary from year to year and month to month.

As I write this, the web site of the Democratic National Committee ["DNC"] has a link to sign up to volunteer: https://my.democrats.org/page/s/volunteer-to-help-democrats-win?source=homepage

The Democratic Congressional Campaign Committee ["DCCC"] works to elect Democrats to the United States House of Representatives. In the past I believe they were more focused on fundraising, but this year they appear to be directly organizing volunteers to get out the vote. You can find them here: https://dccc.org

The Democratic Legislative Campaign Committee ["DLCC"] focuses on electing Democrats to state legislatures. They, too, have become involved in organizing volunteers to increase voter turnout. Here is their web site: http://www.dlcc.org

The Democratic Senate Campaign Committee ["DSCC"], as I write this, does not seem to be directly involved in organizing volunteers. Given the change in the DCCC and the DLCC, that may have changed by the time you read this. They, of course, work to elect Democrats to the United States Senate. You can find them here: http://www.dscc.org

Volunteer with allies of the Democratic Party.

There are allies of the Democratic Party that are often doing this kind of work. Organizations with names like Flippable and Swing Left and Sister District have undertaken to organize volunteers to get out the vote. Democracy for America and MoveOn have organized get out the vote in the past and are likely places to look. If you are a member of a union, that is a likely place to look. There are other organizations that have sprung up in the last couple of years, such as Indivisible, that may be organizing to get out the vote. Here, too, who is actually doing this may vary from year to year and month to month. If there is an organization that you trust and admire and they are doing a GOTV campaign, check it out.

Flippable is an organization that is targeting those state legislative races that have the best chance of gaining a Democratic majority in as many states as possible. Here's what they say: "We maximize our impact by working to flip whole chambers (e.g. a state's Senate or House), not just individual seats. And we focus on states with the worst gerrymandering & voter suppression, because these states have the biggest effect on national politics. In 2018, we're targeting Florida, Pennsylvania, Colorado, Wisconsin, Texas, New Hampshire, Minnesota, Michigan & Arizona." If that sounds like an effort you would like to be a part of, you can find them here: https://www.flippable.org

Swing Left is focused on winning back the House of Representatives. By their analysis, there are 78 seats in the House of Representative that will have competitive races in 2018. To win a majority, Democrats need to pick up 23 seats. They are organizing volunteers, nationally, to increase voter turnout in these targeted districts. To get involved in this effort, go here: https://swingleft.org

Sister District has similar goals. They say, "We organize volunteers into local teams based on where they live, and 'sister' this deep blue energy with swing districts across the country to support strategic state races that matter." "We have a strategic, targeted focus on critical down-ballot, state races that—if we win—will make it easier to win national elections. We support a portfolio of races, with the strategic goals of (1) flipping Republican-held state chambers (2) holding fragile Democratic majorities in state chambers, and (3) making blue inroads in badly gerrymandered states." You can connect with Sister District here: https://www.sisterdistrict.com

Democracy for America and MoveOn have been with us a little longer. Each of them sponsors Democratic candidates in races up and down the ticket. They have often been involved in organizing GOTV efforts. I received some of my first training in how campaigns work from Democracy for America. You can find them here: http://www.democracyforamerica.com

I have fond memories of volunteering with MoveOn to help win back the Congress in 2006. Here is the MoveOn web site: https://front.moveon.org

Postcards to Voters is an organization that … can you guess? If you are ready to write postcards to help get out the vote for Democrats, go to this beautiful web site: https://postcardstovoters.org

When should I volunteer?

Volunteer when you have the time and the motivation.

You are not going to want to miss volunteering in a presidential election campaign. That is an experience you are going to want to have, even if you can only volunteer on the last weekend of the campaign. That is an effort that you are going to want to be a part of. But, as I say, do not wait for that.

The research shows that the smaller the election, the bigger the impact of this kind of work. Why is that?

Presidential elections happen every four years. That is when the most people vote. Every two years there are congressional elections. In the years with congressional elections that are not presidential elections, fewer people vote. Even fewer people vote in the odd years when there are state and local elections but no congressional elections. And even fewer people vote in the special elections that do not happen on a regular election day.

In off-year elections, there is a larger percentage of people who have voted in the past but who, unless they are given a little nudge, might neglect to vote this year. Indeed, that seems to be particularly true for Democrats. That means, the smaller the election, the bigger difference it will make to be giving those little nudges. Each door you knock, each call you make, is more likely to turn out another voter and more likely to swing the election.

Also, as a general proposition, the smaller the election, the fewer the volunteers. That means that each additional volunteer makes a bigger difference in a smaller election.

Each contact that you make will be of the highest priority and will be more likely to have an influence on increasing voter turnout.

Volunteer whenever you have the time and the motivation. Big campaign. Small campaign. Presidential year. Off year. Special elections. It all helps to build that blue wave.

Where do I volunteer?

Here again, you have choices.

First, look to your own neighborhood. The research shows that volunteers can have the biggest impact with the people who know them. Volunteers have the next biggest impact with the people who are most like them. That is likely to be your neighbors. So you might look to a campaign that gives you the opportunity to get out voters in your own neighborhood.

But it does not have to be your neighbors. You might find other places in the city or county or state in which you live.

It might be that in the races that you care about most, your neighborhood is not going to make a difference. You might live in an area where the races are not that close, either an area that is heavily Democratic or an area that is heavily Republican.

Here, too, you have a couple of choices. You can get on the Internet and get on the phone. Campaigns and other organizations getting out the vote will often set up phone banks that you can access through their web sites. You can go to their web site to sign up. Then you can go to their web site and get both a script and numbers to call. If your cell phone lets you call anywhere in the country, you could help key races anywhere. You can do it without leaving home whether you have a little bit of time to give or a lot.

Check out the web site of a particular candidate that you would like to support or of any of the organizations listed earlier in this chapter; they often have an option to volunteer from home no matter where you live.

Or you could travel. Sometimes volunteers will travel on the weekend to spend a couple of days in a neighboring state registering voters or getting out the vote. If you have like-minded friends or a local organization, you can car pool.

Some people are at a point in their lives where they can travel easily. Some are students between terms. Some are retired. Some have jobs that they can do from anywhere. And some will just take some vacation time from work. If this describes you, you might consider traveling to spend a week or two volunteering with a more distant race that inspires you.

I have had some great experiences traveling to help get out the vote in key races. I believe it can be particularly good for the morale of a campaign to have volunteers show up from distant places. You are an inspiration.

"If you came all the way from Oregon to do this, I think I can get myself into the office to do this, too."

"If you came all the way from Oregon to ask me, I think I can get myself the five blocks to my polling place."

Fired up and ready to go?

The bottom line is that you should find a campaign that you are inspired to work on, be it a campaign for a particular candidate or a campaign put together by an organization that is supporting various candidates. If you work with the people that you like and admire the most, you are going to do your best work.

RON BOYER

America was not built on fear. America was built on courage, on imagination and an unbeatable determination to do the job at hand.

Harry Truman

11 THERE IS NO NEWS FROM THE FUTURE

Everyone wants to know in advance how the election is going to turn out. Some people will have predictions. Some of those predictions are more scientific than others. But the truth of the matter is, as Yogi Berra said, "It ain't over 'til it's over."

The truth of the matter is that, until some hours after the polls close, we don't know and we can't know. You can expend a lot of emotional energy and even interpersonal conflict over discussing the question of who is going to win and why you think so. There is no news from the future. Until after the polls close and it is too late to make a difference, we do not know who is going to win.

But there is something that we do know. We know that the kind of work you do in getting out the vote makes a difference. We know that if you do your job and you do it well, we can increase turnout by three to five percent and that is enough to swing a lot of races. We know that if we keep working diligently until the polls close we will improve our chances and we will more races. But we can only do that up until the polls close.

If you recall, going up to the November election in 2016 the best analyses were giving Hillary something like an 80 percent chance of victory. That means that there was a one-in-five chance that she would lose. Whenever you roll a die there is a one-in-six chance that it will come up with a one. And sometimes it does come up a one. That is just the nature of this business.

Sometimes we are faced with a political environment with a real emotional challenge to it. Looking ahead to the November election of 2018 it has sometimes looked this way. Among the congressional races that could go either way, the races that will decide who controls the Congress, there may be just a few races where the Democrat is favored to win. But there might be quite a lot of races where we have a forty percent chance of victory. And here is the good news: if we win forty percent of those races where we have a forty percent chance of victory, we win back the Congress. What that means is we have to put our best effort into all of those races where we have a forty percent chance. Paradoxically, we win back Congress by having sixty percent of our volunteers work on losing races.

That means you really need to keep your spirits up. You have to have faith in the science and faith in your fellow volunteers across the country. You have to not slow down because somebody says that you are probably going to lose the particular race that you are working on. And if you can do that, the odds are in fact very good that we can win back the Congress.

Here is your sports metaphor. Your favorite football team is down by six points and takes over possession with thirty seconds to play deep in their own territory. Do you think the quarterback goes in the huddle and says, "Gee, I don't know, do you think we are going to win?" Or do they go in and say, "Here's what we have to do to win" and then give it their all to do it?

Or suppose it is your favorite team lining up on the other side of the ball. You have got the other team pinned deep in their own territory with thirty seconds left to play. Do you go into the huddle and say, "We've got this game in the bag. I know we are going to win." If you do, you know how that story ends.

Before the polls close we cannot know who is going to win, but we can do things that we know can change the outcome. After the polls close, we can know who won, but we cannot do anything to change the outcome. There will be plenty of time to analyze, to celebrate, to second guess, to mourn after the polls close. Before the polls, just keep your focus on the task at hand. Keep your head when everyone else is losing theirs. Don't get distracted by the news from the future; there is none.

RON BOYER

There is nothing wrong with America that cannot be cured by what is right with America.

Bill Clinton

12 KEEP IT POSITIVE

Find an organization that you are motivated to work for, doing things in a way that you are motivated to do, and then do it. This is a team effort. It is not all that complicated. We have a job to do and we are going to do it together.

Somebody has to be in charge. Usually that is not you. You want to make their job easier, not harder. You might run things differently. But you have got to give the people who are in charge their best chance to try to do things their way.

The paid staff on a campaign with whom volunteers interact may be younger than you and, in some ways, less experienced. And yet they are smart, they are trained, and they will be answering to people who are more experienced. Often the people you will answer to will be college students or fresh out of college. They will also be devoting very long hours at very low pay. Support them. Be kind to them. Treat them with respect.

In everything that you say, in everything that you do, you want to be contributing to the good cheer and positive attitude of the people around you, even when in some way things are going badly. Particularly when things are going badly. If we all do this, things are much more likely to go well.

There will always be some mistakes. There will be misjudgments. There will be omissions. Those will be the exception, not the rule. There is no perfect campaign. At the same time, I believe you will find that the Democratic Party and its allies have taken the quality of voter mobilization campaigns to a pretty high level. I believe you will find that it is a pleasure and an inspiration to work with the other people who show up for these campaigns.

It is often when night looks darkest, it is often before the fever breaks that one senses the gathering momentum for change, when one feels that resurrection of hope in the midst of despair and apathy.

Hillary Clinton

13 WHERE'S THE PARTY?

There's no party until the work is done.

There will be a party. That party will happen sometime after the polls close.

Until the polls close, there will still be volunteers making phone calls, knocking on doors, getting out every last vote. That's where you want to be.

And then there will be tears. Win or lose there will be tears. You will have worked with people who have put their heart and soul into trying to get this election to come out right. When the work is all done, even when we are winning, you can expect a flood of emotion. Even when we are winning, you can expect a flood of exhaustion.

It is a time to express your gratitude to other volunteers. It is a time to comfort people.

I would like to say that we will win every election. I know better.

So, on that election night when you are losing, remember that it is only by pouring our hearts into every election that we win all the elections that we can and should win. It might seem like it would be less painful to only work on winning efforts. But if in every race we do those things that we know how to do to win, including in some races that we are likely to lose, then there are a lot more races that will turn out to be winning efforts.

And you know what is sweet? You want to be there when we win that race that everyone thought we were going to lose. You want to be at the party with the people who make that happen. At that party, you want to be one of the people who made that happen. I am inviting you to that party right now. That is the crest of the wave.

There are no problems we cannot solve together, and very few that we can solve by ourselves.

Lyndon Johnson

WHAT'S MY STORY?

I was born in 1954 in Fort Worth, Texas.

I have worked as a paper boy, a busboy, a ditch digger, a Fuller Brush man, a night manager, a gopher in a law firm, a research assistant to an economist, a library clerk, a teaching assistant, a woodworker, a produce delivery truck driver, a print shop clerk and copy machine operator, a recycling sorter, a laborer, a carpenter, an apple picker, a production line worker in an auto parts plant, a warehouse manager for a vending machine company, a cook in a nursery school, a word processor, a secretary, a legal secretary, a law clerk, and a lawyer. On a couple of occasions I have collected food stamps. I worked 15 years in the Public Defender's Office in Contra Costa County, California, and have worked for about 10 years representing indigent clients in the California Courts of Appeal. I have also briefed and argued a few cases before the California Supreme Court.

In the late 1970s and in the 1980s, I was arrested 10

times in various acts of anti-nuclear and anti-war civil disobedience and spent an aggregate of about six-and-a-half months in various jails and prisons including four months in minimum security at Leavenworth.

I had visited 48 states by the time I was 16. In the 1970s and 1980s, I hitchhiked back and forth across the United States four times and have driven back and forth across the United States a couple more times. I have slept under a bridge in Pennsylvania in the winter time. I have hiked over the Continental Divide in Rocky Mountain National Park. I watched the launch of Apollo 11 from a kayak in the Indian River. I bought the kayak with money from my paper route.

I was educated in public schools in San Diego, California, and Merritt Island, Florida. At Edgewood Junior High School in Merritt Island, Florida, I played contra alto clarinet in the marching band. I was also educated at San Diego City College, Pomona College, Oxford University, the University of Michigan, Stanford University, and the University of California at Berkeley.

The first time I volunteered for a political campaign was in 1972 when I was just shy of 18 years old on Election Day. I drove one voter to the polls for Richard Nixon. Watergate precipitated me out of the Republican Party and I have been a Democrat since.

In 2004 I traveled to Las Cruces, New Mexico, and spent a couple of days getting out the vote for John Kerry.

In 2006 I made get-out-the-vote calls with MoveOn. We were calling for various congressional races across the country. That was a good year.

In 2008, I went back to New Mexico. I asked the Obama campaign where they wanted me and they sent me to Los Alamos of all places. I spent about two weeks knocking on the doors of the scientists and engineers of the national laboratory. And then on Election Day I was a poll watcher assisting with election protection at the Jemez

Pueblo.

In 2010, I helped train canvassers in Richmond, California. It was a hard year for Democrats nationally, but it was a good year for Democrats in California.

In 2012, I started in January as a neighborhood team leader for the Obama Campaign in Albany, California. I organized volunteer phone banks. We were calling battleground states to help get out the vote for Obama and for other Democrats. In the last month or so of the campaign I was a staging location director in Berkeley. We were holding some of the largest phone banks in the State of California. Our main competition was a phone bank that was being held in the old Tower Records Store in the Castro District in San Francisco and the phone bank that was being held in a donated sound stage in Hollywood where celebrities would show up and make calls. We were working out of a building that had been an auto mechanic's garage on San Pablo Avenue and had folding tables set up in the parking lot as well as in the garage.

In 2016 I traveled to Council Bluffs, Iowa, in January and early February to knock on doors and help turn out the vote for the Iowa Caucuses. Then for the rest or the year I organized weekend phone banks for Hillary from my home in Oregon. I also helped to moderate the discussions between volunteers using the on-line call tool of Hillary's campaign.

In March of 2018 I traveled to Greensburg, Pennsylvania, and spent about week knocking doors for Conor Lamb in a special election for Congress.

All of this is possible, in part, because I have a supportive family. I have three grown children, each of whom is a brilliant misfit. I have a particularly supportive wife, also a brilliant misfit, who picks up all the slack when in an election year I might go away for a couple of weeks or might be volunteering locally on multiple weekends. She has even tolerated me organizing phone banks in our house.

I married well. For 25 years I have had an ongoing conversation with her that I feel as though I could have had with no one else. She is a great parent. She is a much better writer than I am. And she is an amazingly talented cook. I know what it is to be lucky. Did I mention that I am so in love with her?

FURTHER READING

If you would like to read more about the research on getting out the vote, you might be interested in:

Get Out the Vote: How to Increase Voter Turnout, by Donald P Green and Alan S. Gerber

The Victory Lab: The Secret Science of Winning Campaigns, by Sasha Issenberg

Mobilizing Inclusion: Transforming the Electorate through Get-Out-the-Vote Campaigns, by Lisa Garcia Bedolla and Melissa R. Michelson.

77554786R00042

Made in the USA
Middletown, DE
22 June 2018